# Selected Poems
## by Gunnar Ekelöf

Translated by
W. H. Auden
and Leif Sjöberg

With an Introduction by
Göran Printz-Påhlson

PANTHEON BOOKS
A Division of Random House, New York

PT
9875
E514
A216
1971

Original Poems Copyright © 1965, 1966 by Gunnar Ekelöf
Translations Copyright © 1967, 1968, 1969, 1970, 1971 by W. H. Auden
and Leif Sjöberg

Forward Copyright © 1971 by W. H. Auden and Leif Sjöberg
Introduction Copyright © 1971 by Göran Printz-Påhlson

Some of these poems originally appeared in
the following publications: *Bennington Review,*
*Denver Quarterly, Michigan Quarterly Review, Mosaic,*
*New York Review of Books, Nimrod, Partisan Review,*
*Poetry Northwest, The Quest, The Sewanee Review, Shenandoah,*
*Southern Humanities Review, Stand, Transatlantic Review.*

ISBN: 0-394-47232-2
Library of Congress Catalog Card Number: 78-177240

Printed and bound by Halliday Lithograph Corp., West Hanover, Mass.

First American Edition

# Contents

# Foreword

Gunnar Ekelöf was born in 1907 in Stockholm. His father was a wealthy stockbroker who caught syphilis, became insane and died while Ekelöf was still a child; his mother was a member of the petty nobility and does not seem to have shown him much affection. Consequently, he had to find such happiness as he could in a private dream world of his own. Of this early time he wrote:

> My own childhood environment was well-to-do but so far beyond the normal and so unrealistic that there was good room for peculiar kinds of want. . . . I had books, music, beautiful furniture around me, but they forced me to go long roundabout ways before I could feel I had a legitimate right to them.

As Ekelöf grew up, he became engrossed in Oriental mysticism:

> I learned to hate Europe and Christianity and during the morning prayer at school I began to mumble *Om mani padme hum* as a form of protest . . .

In the Royal Library he discovered *Tarjúmán el-Ashwáq* by Ibn el-Arabi which for a long time was his favourite book and from which, he tells us, he first learned what is meant by Symbolism and Surrealism. With the idea of emigrating to India, he went to London to study at the School of Oriental Languages, but abandoned this scheme and returned to Sweden to study Persian at the University of Uppsala. However, a long illness prevented him from completing his studies. It was at this time that he wrote his first poem:

> One night I had an experience that I would have to characterize

as a form of ecstasy. It came over me as a shower of shooting stars, and I remember staggering a bit on my way home. As often on such occasions, I had had the usual orchestra playing somewhere behind me, and I myself joined in with one instrument after the other. Then it became a poem, my first fairly original one.

Ekelöf's second great and lasting passion was music and, in the 1920s, he went to Paris to study it, but soon became absorbed by the problems of poetic language:

> I placed one word beside another and finally with a great deal of effort managed to construct a whole sentence – naturally not one that 'meant something' but one that was composed of word-nuances. It was the hidden meaning that I was seeking – a kind of *Alchemie du verbe*. One word has its meaning and another word has its own, but when they are brought together something strange happens to them: they have an in-between connotation at the same time as they retain their original individual meanings ... poetry is this very tension-filled relationship between the words, between the lines, between the meanings.

It was in Paris, it would seem, that he wrote many of the poems which appeared in his first book, *Sent på jorden* (*Late on the Earth*), which was published in 1932. This he later described as a 'suicidal book':

> I literally used to walk around with a revolver in my pocket. Illegally, for that matter. In my general despair I did everything possible to remain in my dream-world – or to be quickly removed from it. I began to gamble and I lost my money, which made my temporary return to Sweden quite definite.

*Late on the Earth* attracted little critical attention, but by the time of the publication of *Färjesång* (*Ferry Song*) in 1941, he had become recognized as one of Sweden's leading poets.

The translations in this Penguin volume are of two late works, *Dīwān över Fursten av Emgión* (*Dīwān over the Prince of Emgión*), 1965, and *Sagan om Fatumeh* (*The Tale of*

*Fatumeh*), 1966. His last volume, *Vägvisare till underjorden* (*Guide to the Underworld*) was published in 1967. In 1968 he died of cancer of the throat.

The Prince of Emgión had appeared in two earlier poems. Ekelöf relates that, during a spiritualist seance in Stockholm during the thirties, he had asked where his spiritual 'I' was to be found. The oracle, a drinking-glass placed upside down, replied: 'In Persia and his name is the Prince of Emgión.' Later, Ekelöf came to believe that this Prince was of Armenian-Kurdish stock, half a Christian and half a Gnostic.

*Dīwān* was begun in Constantinople in 1965, and most or all of the poems were written within a period of four weeks. '*Dīwān*,' Ekelöf wrote to a friend, 'is my greatest poem of love and passion. I cannot touch it nor see it because I grow ill when I see this blind and tortured man. . . . As far as I can understand, someone has written the poems with me as a medium. . . . Really, I have never had such an experience, or not one as complete.'

The character he here refers to is not the Prince, but Digenís Acrítas, the hero of an eleventh-century Byzantine epic romance. Digenís was the son of an Arab father and a Byzantine mother. Captured in battle, he was incarcerated in the prison of Vlacherne, where he was tortured and blinded. In his suffering his principal consolation is the Virgin, to whom he addresses passionate hymns. Though there are references to what are obviously Christian icons, this figure is not the Christian Madonna, but rather the Earth Mother, the Goddess known to us through St Paul as the 'Diana of the Ephesians'. In *Dīwān* another female figure appears who is human, not divine, perhaps a wife, perhaps a sister or daughter.

*The Tale of Fatumeh* is an equally sad story. It tells of a

9

generous, loving girl who becomes first a courtesan and then the beloved of a prince, whose child she bears; she is apparently deserted by him and brought to the Harem at Erechtheion, but she is eventually thrown out of the Harem and spends a miserable old age, selling herself to keep alive. Like Digenís, Fatumeh is sustained by her visions. Whatever has happened and may happen, no disaster shall degrade her soul.

Like the Greek poet Constantine Cavafy, Ekelöf sets these poems in a bygone age. Different in sensibility as they are – Cavafy is ironic and detached, Ekelöf passionate and involved – neither chooses the past as an escape: for both it is a means for illuminating and criticizing the present. Although Ekelöf was fascinated by Byzantium, he never idealized it. 'Why,' he wrote in a letter, 'have I become interested in the Byzantine, the Greek life? Because Byzantine life, traditionally and according to deep-rooted custom, is like the political life in *our* cities and states. I am intensely interested in it because I hate it. I hate what is Greek. I hate what is Byzantine. . . . *Dīwān* is a symbol of the political decadence we see around us. *Fatumeh* is a symbol of the degradation, the coldness between persons, which is equally obvious.'

Ekelöf had a special numerological theory and considered life an odd number and death an even number. His numerological preoccupation is expressed in his division of *The Tale of Fatumeh* into a *naẓm*, a string of beads, and a *tesbiḥ*, a rosary, each consisting of twenty-nine numbered poems. This plan regrettably had to be abandoned for this version. Some textual emendations have also been made whenever Ekelöf's manuscripts have warranted such action.

W. H. AUDEN
LEIF SJÖBERG

# Works by Gunnar Ekelöf

*Sent på jorden* (poems), 1932; *Hundra år modern fransk dikt* (translations), 1934; *Dedikation* (poems), 1934; *Sorgen och stjärnan* (poems), 1936; *Köp den blindes sång* (poems), 1938; *Promenader* (essays), 1941; *Färjesång* (poems), 1941; *Non Serviam* (poems), 1945; *Utflykter* (essays), 1947; *Dikter I–III* (collected poems), 1949; *Om hösten* (poems), 1951; *Strountes* (poems), 1955; *Dikter 1932–1951* (collected poems), 1956; *Blandade kort* (essays), 1957; *Verklighetsflykt* (selected essays), 1958; *Opus Incertum* (poems), 1959; *Valfrändskaper* (translations), 1960; *En Mölna-elegi* (poem), 1960; *En natt i Otočac* (poems), 1961; *Sent på jorden med Appendix 1962 och En natt vid horisonten, 1930–1932* (poems), 1962; *Dikter* (collected poems), 1965; *Dīwān över Fursten av Emgión* (poems), 1965; *Sagan om Fatumeh* (poems), 1966; *Vatten och sand* (selected poems), 1966; *Vägvisare till underjorden* (poems), 1967; *Urval* (selections of poems 1928–68), 1968; *Lägga patience* (essays), 1969; *Partitur* (a selection of unpublished poems 1965–8), 1969.

# Introduction

This selection emphasizes the paradoxical exoticism of Ekelöf's last phase: a Swedish poet almost exclusively pre-occupied with conjuring up the Orient. The two volumes represented here are wholly given to a self-contained and painstakingly faithful re-creation of a bygone reality, so obtrusively objective that Ekelöf even claimed that the first book had been 'dictated' to him. Those who are familiar with the history and poetry of the peoples of the Near and Middle East in early medieval times will recognize the almost uncanny accuracy of both fact and tone.

This was not a new preoccupation of Ekelöf's, although he re-established his ties with Greece and the Middle East in the mid sixties. After all, he read Oriental Languages as a young student at both Uppsala and London in the twenties. There are many other poems of his – in particular from his middle period – which are thoroughly steeped in Oriental tradition and lore. It may seem a little quaint to the English reader – like Borges's preoccupation with the Nordic tradition – but it is, after all, not unique. The smaller literatures are often devoted to that Romantic tradition of 'universal poetry' which Friedrich Schlegel so convincingly advocated. In Swedish literature, for instance, at the high noon of the Romantic era, among all the bardic Norse war-whoops, was a poet as thoroughly obsessed by Oriental and Early Christian mystic traditions as Ekelöf: E. J. Stagnelius, whom Ekelöf has edited and written about.

Yet the almost complete identification in the Emgión and Fatumeh poems is a different matter. The psychological problems involved here are considerable and shed light on interesting contradictions within the modernist tradition.

To elucidate these, and also to justify the claim that Ekelöf's poetry is important, which would hardly be so if he were just a clever *pasticheur*, we must scrutinize his earlier poetry and his peculiar development.

In the cultural and historical preoccupations of his poetry Ekelöf is closer to the first Modernists – Eliot, Pound, Stevens – than he is to his exact English contemporaries of the thirties – Auden, Spender or MacNeice. In the period when English poetry was given to the large political gesture and the wry social comment, Ekelöf was busy exploring the inner recesses of his mind and his relationship to a native Swedish Romantic tradition.

His early poetry was strongly influenced by Surrealism. He wrote his first volume of poems in Paris and introduced the French Surrealists into Sweden. He seems to have been particularly fascinated, not by any of the major figureheads of the movement, but by a rather marginal outsider, Robert Desnos. He also translated poems from the then re-discovered nineteenth-century precursors of Surrealism, Rimbaud and Lautréamont. But he rejected most of both the philosophy and the techniques of Surrealism, which seemed to him lifeless and arid. Although his own poetic method depends utterly on spontaneity and the uncon-scious, he considered both psychoanalysis and the automatic writing of Surrealism too mechanical, too rational. Dreams and madness seemed to promise more. The personal crisis resulting in his first volume of poetry, the 'suicidal book' *Late on the Earth*, was of a kind that would not relinquish its grip even after he had outwardly overcome it. The rich-ness of the experience, obtrusive, undeniable, was to haunt his poetry for decades. He continually reverted to the poems of this period in different phases of his later development, trying to restore them to a form closer to the original

14

inspiration and also evidently using them as a source of strength and insight. Ekelöf's revision of his early poetry would be worth close inspection; his motives are clearly different from those prompting Yeats or Auden to alter and rewrite. In his obsession with spontaneity there is an element of primitivism, although of a quaint, curiously antiquated type, which shows more affinity with the Stoic philosophers than with Rousseau. The Golden Age has vanished, but we can always hope to re-establish some tenuous link with the inner resources which made it possible. In order to do this we have to erase, layer by layer, the cultural sediment which hinders us.

This seems to be Ekelöf's main preoccupation in his poetry of the forties and early fifties, which is also his most conventional. 'Conventional', that is, in the sense of being concerned with the conventions and preconditions of human life, rather than in the sense of being 'unoriginal'. He forms a dialectical view of human reason and psychology, revitalizing the old concept of a *coincidentia oppositorum*, and he introduces the idea of man as a composite being, torn asunder by conflicting elements. Some of his most impressive philosophical and psychological poems date from this period. The most memorable of his always subtly varied images is that of *Archaeopteryx*, the fossil bird imprisoned in stone, living matter in hard rock.

Unlike Eliot or Pound, Ekelöf has no vision of a great cross-cultural synthesis. Instead of laboriously tracing discordant personal echoes down the corridors of History, he sees the poetic process as one of erasure, a gradual discarding of layer after layer of cultural sediment. Nowhere has he expressed this idea in more arresting and moving words than in one of the late poems, *Xoanon*, included in this volume. Its theme is the slightly obscene, lovingly slow stripping of an icon:

I remove the gold ground and the ground coat
Until the thick-veined wood is exposed
A piece of old olive wood, saved long ago
Out of a storm-felled tree
On some coast way up in the north. In the wood
Almost hidden, an eye, the eye-knot of a twig
That must have been broken off when the tree was still young

This is the only way to reach what is truly human, what is common to man. And those who dare to do so find that they are not alone; instead, they are intently watched.

One also has to see Ekelöf's technical development as a result of this urge to erase, to deprive his own poetry of any cultural privileges. It could be called a democratic urge, since it seems to involve a vision of the basic equality of man. His poetry of the late fifties and early sixties was dominated by this impulse to create a style simplified almost to the point of meaninglessness: short poems, many of them built on grotesque puns, obscene palindromes, a sort of Dadaist stutter, but influenced by the classical *graffiti* from Pompeii and Herculaneum that he was studying at the time.

In the long run, it was impossible for Ekelöf to be satisfied with this weird diction (which has, incidentally, exerted a great and not always beneficial influence on younger Swedish poets). It must have seemed to him too contrived, paradoxically too literary, in its absolute claim to artlessness. His last phase was the Byzantine trilogy where he abandoned himself to the absolute sincerity of the pastiche. Needless to say, he was not successful in banishing his personality or his mastery of language. Like Pierre Mesnard, in the story by Borges, who aspired to rewrite *Don Quixote* exactly as it had once been written, Ekelöf was helpless to erase his own personal imprint from his poetry.

Why is Ekelöf worth reading? Why have so many out-standing writers translated and commented on his work: Nelly Sachs, Hans Magnus Enzensberger, Jean-Clarence Lambert, Octavio Paz, Robert Bly, Muriel Rukeyser, and now W. H. Auden? Martin Dodsworth has put the case against translating poetry succinctly:

> One aspect of a poem's translatability is its language: the more it exploits the particular qualities of its own language, the less available that poem is for translation.

If we value poetry for its linguistic complexity, then the art of translation has a bleak future. But I am not so sure about Ekelöf. His language is difficult and complex, no doubt. But in the hard-won simplicity of these later poems, in particular, there is a moral strength that transcends the complexity. It seems to me that these poems are eminently translatable, not because they are inherently simple, or rely on simple images or symbols, but because of the urgent conviction behind them, the painstaking will to expression. They are borne by a voice, a *breathing*, strangely muted, almost passionately expressionless, like Ekelöf's reading voice, which is unmistakable and unforgettable.

It is the heroes and champions of subjective poetry, like Wordsworth or Whitman, who have mostly striven to incorporate their own personal development in their poetic achievement. In the case of Ekelöf, we have a strange reversal of this tendency. In his quest for a depersonalized poetry and a depersonalized experience, for a poem which is deprived of all literary trimmings, which has erased everything that is not basically human, he managed, in the end, to write his own biography.

The last poem in the recently published posthumous collection, *Partitur*, written during Ekelöf's painful final illness, states with extreme simplicity that he 'rests his case on nothingness'. This pained insight reveals, I think, more a clarity of mind than any despair. Ekelöf remained throughout – like the Digenís Acrítas he refers to in his late poetry – a Twiceborn Borderer, claiming a double heritage of culture and nature, or humanity and despair, a guardian of the border regions of the mind. We can hear his sardonic message to posterity in an earlier poem (trans. Muriel Rukeyser and Leif Sjöberg):

The classical record spins, we must help it over the circular grooves where it sticks and spins for itself. The human hit parade breaks through. *Yes Posthumus I am signing off now.*

GÖRAN PRINTZ-PÅHLSON

# Dīwān over the Prince of Emgión

This poem of mine is without rhyme: I intend by it
only Her.
The word 'Her' is my aim, and for Her sake I am
not fond of bartering except with 'Give' and 'Take'.

*Tarjúmán el-Ashwáq*, XLII

In my dreams I heard a voice:
– Ḥabīb, would you like this onion
Or just a slice of it?
At this I fell into great disquiet
This enigmatic question
Was the question of my life!
Did I prefer the part to the whole
Or the whole to the part
No, I wanted both
The part of the whole as well as the whole
And that this choice would involve no contradiction.

I speak to you
I speak of you
From deep within myself
I know that you do not answer
How could you answer
When so many are crying out to you!
All I ask is permission
To stand here waiting
And that you will give me a sign
From within myself of yourself!

Upright alone
You stand in the blue
Of the Night-sky
Without a child
Your own Fate
Six-winged Cherubim
Stand watch about you
And I the heavy-laden
Prince of Emgión
Here on a mountain
This mountain named 'Humility'.

I see you afar off
Rising out of the Seas of Smoke
In a strictly-pleated robe
You do not see me

But You, Stranger
I strive to reach you
Row towards you
Like a man with only one oar
At the other gunwale perhaps
Someone stronger is pulling
In the struggle my hands lose their grip
The boat goes round and round
In the circles of Day and Night
But never do I lose my grip upon You.
You
Shall be my oar!

Nothing, You tender and merciful One
Who place men's hands in one another
For equilibrium
Who have flowers in your finger-tips
And touch me like a breath
Of all my senses
The fragrance of your skin
Your voice, your caress
Is stronger at the edge of You.

# enýpnion*

– About what has befallen me
Never ask

Then she carefully wraps me
In a white garment
Gives me a sip of Moorish wine
And lays me to rest
Between weathering rocks.

* *Enýpnion*: can be roughly translated as a dreamlike slumber,
things that one sees in a dream.

I feel your arms around me
Invisible but present.
You allowed me to kiss
One of your breasts
The one over your heart
Then you left me
After kissing my eyelids.

# *enýpnion**

She sleeps in her mantle
Who? The soul, the soul of a man
What fate is seeking her?
A natural star descends
To the sleeper
His soul becomes mother
To other sleepers –

Help me to wake up
Wisest of concierges
Who sleeps so lightly
With the string of the bell around your wrist

Help me to wake up!
I dreamed of rape –
She prompted your dream!
I dreamed of a caress –
She inspired your dream
She who pulls the string
That rocks the cradle
She prompted your sleep.

 * See note, page 26.

Could I
Describe Height
I would choose blue
And two flecks of Gold:
A star at the head
A star at the feet
And under the feet a mirror-image
Concluding in a star

Could I describe breadth
I would choose an embrace
Because I have senses
False and primitive
And cannot grasp what really Exists –
There is no Star
Where your Head is
There is no Middle-point
Where your feet stand
But an inch of your loveliness
I have known.

You who have the strength
To be yielding
Not to desire
Not to Exist

Who does not love you
Who sets us free from love
Birth, pain and death!

Outside, I should like to see
Your Inside
Was it red? Was it white?
Outside, show me your Inside!
Is it white? Is it red?
Outside, are you brave enough?
Inside, are you brave?
Tell me what disguise you wear
How you paint yourself so white and so red
That your cheeks should be so lovely
Your feet so small
As to be barely visible
Under your flowered robe.

I saw them
In the sandals which trod on me
But which when I had unloosed the sandals
Caressed me as I did them –
First the fine long toe
Ahead of the big toe
Then the others in their beautiful sequence

Still the Arch of your foot is mine
And its narrow-edged Heel
Which is like a sword
With a ruddy hue on the steel.

No, the Merciful He, the Merciful She
give no bread, give no breast, give no water
No night-lodging no marriage-bed
She does not give, she cannot give
And in this she is honest
The Merciful She gives what she does not give
What she could not or would not give

That Gift is called Distance
You who are strong in love
You were there
And passed quietly by.

A bullet have I cast for you
To shoot you in my heart
It is made of stone, quarried by convicts
It is lead, dipped in blood
It is iron, dipped in honey
It is a hacked-out lump of ore
With jagged edges
To make worse wounds
To make you feel
What it means to die of love.

In through the grating flew a bird's feather
The wind carried it here
Or else somebody carried it
It lay on the floor for a long time
Before I cradled it in my hands
– A common dove's feather

Now I will tell you a prisoner's secret:
Not all doves are common!

Out of love and loving desire
To lose consciousness
At the mere sound of a voice
At the sound of a guzla*
Of such things the old tales tell us
I know it can really happen
That beauty is a weapon
Which fells princes to the ground –

How long does the faintness last?
An eternity, and then
One awakes in another time
And looks around with astonishment –
What is such an eternity?
I know. One thousand and one heart-beats
And then one awakes in the same world
But the mark left is indelible
It was not your foot I yearned for
But your foot in Hers
Whose footsteps lead towards Nothing.

* *Guzla*: a stringed instrument.

36

*ayíasma**

A one-eyed prison-warder
In charge of the hidden
Sacred well
Gives us water
To pour over our hands
The same water that purified
Mad emperors tormented
By power and suspicion
O filthy lust after power!

I was with Romanós
Beheld the slaughter and the treachery
O filthy lust after power!
Water to cleanse our hands –
Surely even this
The simplest of actions
Can cleanse our hands from all they desired to seize
Our simple hands:
From lust after power from lust after lust –

You say: I am innocent
Because all is possible –

This possible evil
Was sufficient according to our measure.

 * *Ayíasma* (Hagíasma): purifying well. 'The water cult is still
alive in Greece and the Near East. A glass of cold water is the holy
welcoming drink among the people.'

# *ayiasma**

In the calm mirror I saw mirrored
Myself, my soul:
Many wrinkles
The beginnings of a turkey-cock neck
Two sad eyes
Insatiable curiosity
Incorrigible pride
Unrepentant humility
A harsh voice
A belly slit open
And sewn up again
A face scarred by torturers
A maimed foot
A palate for fish and wine
One who longs to die
Who has lain with some
In casual beds – but for few
Has felt love – a for him
Necessary love
One who longs to die
With someone's hand in his
Thus I see myself in the water
With my soiled linen left behind me when I am gone
A Kurdic Prince called a dog
By both Rumaians† and Seldjuks
In the water my bald forehead:
All the mangled tongues
Which have convinced me

* See note, page 37.
† Descendants of a Roman population in the Balkans.

That I am mute
And those stains on my shirt
Which water will never wash out –
Indelible like blood, like poison
The stains of the heretic
Shall strike them like the plague
With still blacker stains.

The one revealed to you:
A six-winged being
With black white feathers
Double sex
And enigmatic face
Looked intently at you –

Born from an explosion
Of red-hot needles in the light of my eyes
– Who then kissed
The shut and painful eyelid?
Someone who was No One!
I know: a Daughter.
On our way to Smyrna, Manisa, Sart
Qonia and over the mountains,
Frat, and again over the mountains
To pastures I shall never see
Blinded led by a blind one
By a blind one who leads another
Whose eyes have been put out
One whom I call my daughter
Leads a blinded man who sees.

Are you lonely
So be it!
You will acquire a great train
In the end.

# ayiasma*

The black image
Framed in silver worn to shreds by kisses
The black image
Framed in silver worn to shreds by kisses
Framed in silver
The black image worn to shreds by kisses
Framed in silver
The black image worn to shreds by kisses
All round the image
The white silver worn to shreds by kisses
All round the image
The very metal worn to shreds by kisses
Framed in metal
The black image worn to shreds by kisses
The Darkness, O, the darkness
Worn to shreds by kisses
The Darkness in our eyes
Worn to shreds by kisses
All we wished for
Worn to shreds by kisses
All we never wished for
Kissed and worn to shreds by kisses
All we escaped
Worn to shreds by kisses
All we wish for
Kissed again and again.

* See note, page 37.

Lady richest in all things
In chastity in unchastity
Richest in beauty
In companionship, in loneliness
Why, you disguise yourself
As a beggar-woman
Sitting on the pavement
Holding your hand out

To you I have given
The silver coin which was yours
Concealed under the copper coin
Which was mine.

Lady of Consolation
You who have No One
Who expect no one
Whose little face
Peeps out from the blanket –
You who have all
Mother to all
Therefore to no one
Whose breasts are sufficient for all
Alone
You who are outside all men
The only one for all.

# The Logothete's Annotation*

The Prince of Emgión
Lived here for four or five years
He was Lord of the Marches
And not to be trusted.
He was even suspected of sympathizing
With the doomed Vasilévs Romanós and his party.
His wife or was it his daughter prayed for him
With heart and soul.
In the times of trouble
Before Nikifóros Votaniátes was deposed
He was released
But only after his eyes had been put out.
He had succumbed to the Manichaean heresy.

* *Logothétis* (Logothete): the Emperor's minister, councillor. He
is supposed to have made the ironic annotation about the Prince of
Emgión. In Greece the punishment of blinding was as old as the
myth of Oedipus.

The story of the blinded one's love.
Once he was a Prince
Who ruled over many
But loved horses best
Then he was blinded
With red-hot needles.
He said: a greater light I never saw
Than this red-hot glow
Nor a greater darkness!
But I taught my hands to see
Another light
The light of touch.

He if anyone
Could feel almost hear
From your voice
If you were young
If you were old
If you were beautiful
If you were wise.

I still live in Constantinople
If you call it living
A Kurdic Prince of the tribe
Whose pasture-lands lie above the Van

For three days, three nights I have lain
On this clay dug out of the floor
For three days
Warmed it with my body
Moistened it with my urine
Kneaded it with my faeces
That dry hard
Out of their mass to shape their names
In Persian letters
Which they cannot read.

In summer suffering from thirst
Thirst is longing
For what lives in the light
That filters in through the grating
In winter suffering from cold
And the water on the floor
Which makes my feet swell up
Suffering from hunger suffering from fear
That something may be happening up there
In the most secret chambers
Of the Emperor's palace
Which will cause me to be forgotten
And always suffering from love
Which rises only to sink
Which awakes and shivers

Should they forget me
I shall soon be a skeleton
Standing there scrabbling at the wall
With broken nails.

Overhead
I hear water organs
Squeaking of flutes and throbbing of drums
Nikifóros!
When you are not pondering questions of dogma
Or the balance of power between Logothete and
    Metropolitan
Ponder ways by which you may escape being poisoned
And eye this body-guard with trust
That with suspicion
As you dance overhead
Like Solomon dancing before the altar of the Lord
I can hear a harsher sound
A goatherd piping in the mountains
Women keening at somebody's death
You are dancing over our head
I shall never dance over yours
It will lie forgotten
In a nameless grave.

The devil is god
God is the devil
And I was taught
To worship them both
One in this way
The other in that
Yet both ways were the same
For both were tyrants
Until I became aware of
Love, a chink
Between the two locked in combat
Love, a chink
Of light between their bloody lips
The gap through which the chosen can enter
The world where it is all one
All one if they worship a God
All one if they worship a Devil.

The Devil is a great prophet
Equally great is God
And between them is war
On both sides it is only a matter of enduring courage
Of sheer endurance
– Of who can hold out longest!

But over those
Who huddle together low in morale
Sons of God and Sons of the Devil
Stands she who is Mother to no man
But who has breasts
With milk for all.

Digenís is dead
Greatest of the Lords of the Marches
And Eudokía
A noble, worthy follower
On his chest
Who will now oppose the eunuchs
And their armies
On this bank of the Euphrates?
It is better to deny
The god who does not exist
And instead to worship in secret
The virgin who does
Better the Arab's handshake
The gift of a stallion
Than the Logothete's promise

She, the virgin, will still visit you
In the guise of a young girl
Can you not feel her arms around you.


*In memory of 'Angelos Sikelianós*

To ambush and kill
Would not have become me
I myself was ambushed and taken prisoner,
And they are killing me slowly,
Extremely slowly.

Had I met you, Digenís,
We would have laid down our weapons
And embraced each other,
Talked long with each other
About what we should fight over this day
And, even as we parted, embraced each other.

To himself –
As tamer of horses, as cup-bearer,
Yes, and as watcher over the tulips in his garden
Where he loved to sit
And interpret the speech of birds –
The Emperor Babr brought my son
To the highlands of Ferghana
I have not heard of him since
But everyone knows what has happened –
I too loved to sit in my garden
Listening as Persian poems were read to me
I was no less a Prince than he
A King over shepherds
As much an Arab as he a Turk or a Greek
A conqueror of kingdoms

About the mother something is known among us
About the father almost nothing
Christians have told me
That something is known about the father
But almost nothing about the mother
A blasphemous lie
Babr became Emperor
And I was blinded
From my son I have heard nothing
From my daughter I have learned
That high up above us

High in the blue
Stands a lonely daughter, not sold
And with no child
She gives herself to no one
She can be taken by anyone.

Why did Digenís send me
As a hostage
Who is himself a half-breed
Why did not Eudokía speak
But she was dying
Wholly engrossed with themselves
Are those dying
They cannot think of others
Cannot afford to think
Even of themselves
Contending with life
Contending with death
As I do.

My heart is disquieted within me
Its trouble invades my hands
My stiffening member
My throbbing temples
Goddess
My Mother
Who is also my Daughter
Kiss these blinded eyes
Kiss them with a dream
As has been your wont

Lay your hand on my heart
Light as the caress of a bird's wing
So that it may be stilled
Let it only beat
In adoration before you
Let my heart beat
Standing upright with lifted hands
In your service.

The executioner made me bleed
I did not feel it
Shamefully violated me
Racked out my genitals
To three times their length
And twisted them
Into a three-stranded rope
Of skin, of screams

But my sex, executioner,
Is not between my legs
My senses, executioner,
Which betrayed fictitious names
Are not in my senses, executioner,
It is in my heart, executioner,
Stab deeply, executioner,
And twist
All you will learn
Is that it has taken flight
From all its betrayals
My heart
Was not even in my heart
It grew wings.

In the yard of the common soldiers
I have seen a thousand and one stinking heads
Brought in from various parts of the country
And piled up in a pyramid
Like so many cannon-balls
But these no longer suffer
They are merely dead
Why then should I speak of my torments?
But I shall! Yes, their bodies rest
Delivered from all evil
I am alive
Alive in the seeds of hatred
That our wives and daughters
Through their funeral dirges
Transmit to their children.
How then can I do anything but love you
Childless mother
Of us all.

## ayiasma*

Give me water
Not to drink
But to wash myself in
I do not ask for oil
Give me fresh water

See how worms multiply in my arm-pits
On my left thigh on my right
And in between
Boils suppurate
I can pull the skin off the soles of my feet
Give me your water to wash myself in
Not your oil
Your oil I reject
Give me water.

　* See note, page 37.

Like women returning
With jars on their heads or shoulders
From gossiping by the well
Full of each other
Of their neighbours' husbands and sons
Full of themselves
Lift your jar from head or shoulder
Set it down
And give a thought to one
Whose throat is choked with dust
Who has not eaten or drunk for three days
Think of me and what has befallen me
Not only of your neighbour and your neighbour's
    neighbour
Give me water from your hands, my daughter
I cannot even see to drink.

Your water can purify the Outside
Nobody is unstained
By ill-deeds done in the world
But the Inside it purifies even better
It deadens your hunger
Kills the worms that gnaw
The bread on which you live
When there is any bread
Soothes inflamed eyes
That have seen everything
And now only remember
What once they saw

You will never see anything more
Than what you have seen
But gaze inwardly !
Most of what you saw
You never saw
Now again it comes back to you.

That I should go outside myself
Who have only myself to be in
Is *that* what you demand!
Cannot you see the blood-stain
On the clay floor
Oozing in the corner:
Not long ago my cell was flooded
Three days and nights I stood
In water up to my waist
Before it sank and I could lie in it and rest
My head on soaked and rotting straw.

Lead me, Princess, by the hand
Come let us go now
Through the Fertile Crescent
Back to our native land

No one can harm us
And we harm no one

To have been blinded sharpens the vision
Till all is light
The light of memory.

I let the barber cut away
What was left of my eyes
And sear away the pus
With a hot iron

This is the land of the blind singers
There have been many like them
My wife leads me by the hand
And I have cut myself a stick
Who now remembers that we were Princes?
Yet even such birds She feeds
With barely adequate food
Like the birds I still hear singing
Hearing now what once I saw.

On the road to Sardes
She tells me what she sees
Caves and ruined walls in the mountains
An image carved in the rock
Of whom by whom
I do not know
She says there is snow on the mountains
As if I did not feel it
She says the peasants wear dresses of many colours
As if I did not know it
This is the King's Highway
Which runs through the winter
To the Fertile Crescent
Then on from there climbs upwards
Into my native land, towards the Star in the bow of the
    crescent moon
Into a new winter
There I want to listen to the silence of the brooks
The mountain brooks
So that once again I may hear the murmur.

*ná tin Nióvin*

Niobe weeps for her children
And with good reason, no doubt
Murdered by the gods of men
The thoughts of men
The gods personified

She weeps for them
Huge in the Magnetic Rock
She weeps for them
Beside the road to Sardes
Crying stone
Great Mother
Ancient as the night-sky
The stars we see with our eyes
Are her tears
All the rest she herself
Night's real face
Is eroded by those tears
And impersonal.

To walk in rags
With unwashed hands
And soiled feet
Blinded
My scrotum cut off
And the glans of my member
A scar over my heart
However, they have not dared to stab me in the back
I have always turned towards them
Mutilated
I walk led by my daughter
Who perhaps is my sister
Towards the mountains
I can hear them smell
I can feel them rise.

## To Nizám

A blind man able to feel happy
At what others tell me they see
This has been my gain
To feel this hand in mine
Calloused from picking edible herbs
But still very young
Too young perhaps
Sometimes when she is away
– I know why –
And I sit on a stone here waiting for her
I can tell from feeling
The various leaves and grasses around me
How differently each of them smells
This gives me back something of what I used to see. Yes –
Once I rode a stallion
Of Shammar stock
From the stud of the Prophet
And took small interest in girls

I can hear
The big bronze bell of the leading goat
And the bells of the camel train
From the big bell of the first one
To the little bell of the eighth and hindmost –
I can hear the steps
Of passers-by
I remember and I therefore know
That I am not blind
Only blinded
I used to see

And I can read the girl's mind
From the way she holds my hand
When tightly I know she knows
When less tightly I know she is afraid.

This you know and ought to know:
A daughter can be her husband's father
Her father's father
And a man can be his daughter's mother
He may be unfaithful
He may be blind

But if you have a good daughter
Cherish her
Make much of her
If you let her go
No matter how great the marriage portion
You will quickly grow old
And sit there with your worthless money
Alone

Do not sell her
Give her away
To the man you love
And for whom she feels no aversion.

O narrow chink
Between good and evil
You who know nothing of shame
You who know only what is afar off
Just as a girl of fourteen
And betrothed wearing
A crown of turquoises knows
What is afar off

To you shall no god come
No man no Spirit
And no Demon
For you are holy in yourself
Your breasts shall become innumerable
For your daughters' breasts
Also shall give us milk
Mysterious you shall stand
Aloft in the sky
Your eyes like stars
Shall beam upon the flocks
Of us who are shepherds

The young men
Shall dance foot to foot
The young girls
Veil their faces
Both out of mutual desire
But you shall remain unattainable
You shall remain the one.

You who came upon me
In the day of my affliction
What can I give you
That I too can see with my hands
Rings of gold
Or just a single ring
In the lobe of the ear, or a moonstone in the nostril
Perhaps a barber-surgeon
Could sew a thread of pure silver
Into the cleft between your breasts
And hang from it an image of me
If an image of one who is invisible cannot be made
He may hang there a mirror!

Round two of your toes
You shall wear little rings of gold
Which I can touch but not see
And on your forehead a crown
Of golden coins
And I shall tell you, no sing
Stories, no! – songs
So that in my mind
I shall see your eyes grow dark
And in the depth of your eyes
A red lustre of wine
And round their rims
A ring of pure water

My annunciation
In the day of my affliction
Let us sleep
Each alone
Close to each other.

Our talk on the road
Between Water and Thirst
Makes me remember
The blossoming days of my youth

I said to myself:
After fifty years
When through self-reflection and doubt
I have become as helpless as a fledgling bird
I am reminded of the road
Between the watering-troughs 'Yes!' and 'No!'
And how we drove our camels uphill and downdale
And how I kindled watch-fires for them
By rubbing sticks
Of the tree Nothing
And the tree Something
Against each other.

# The Tale of Fatumeh

In the autumn or the spring –
What difference does that make?
In youth or in old age –
What does it matter?
In any case You disappear
Into the image of the Whole
You have vanished, You vanished
Now or the moment before
Or a thousand years ago
But Your disappearance
Remains.

## The Tale of Fatumeh

Five times I saw the Shadow
And greeted her as we passed
But the sixth time
In a narrow alley of the lower city
Suddenly she stood before me
Barring my way
And began to revile me
In the coarsest language –
Then she asked me:
'Why have you rejected me?
Why have you not lain with your Shadow?
Am I so repulsive?'
To which I answered:
'How can a man lie with his Shadow?
It is customary
To let it walk two paces behind me
Until the evening'
She smiled scornfully
And pulled her black shawl tighter about her face:
'And after sunset?'
'Then the wanderer has two shadows,
One from the lantern he has just left behind him
And one from the lantern he is just approaching:
They keep changing places'
She smiled scornfully and laid her hand on the
    neighbouring wall:
'Then I am not your Shadow?'
I said: 'I do not know whose shadow you are'
And meant to walk on
But, lifting her hand, she showed its black impression

In the moonlight on the white wall
And said again:
'Then I am not your Shadow?'
To which I answered:
'I see who you are.
It is for you to take me
Not for me to take you'
She smiled scornfully. 'Beloved,' she said
'At your place? Or at mine?'
'At yours,' I answered.

As if the sea followed me
And flung its arms around me
In my room, in the night
– As if the sea wrapped around me
Its arms of sounds
The sea grips me
The sea embraces me.

Mother, I know to what you sold me:
It was to the High Gate
Which is called Death
There in its world of mirrors
I shall meet myself
As a child of myself
With the songs you taught me
With beauty, with tales
With deep looks, with milk
With the smell of the sweat of my wet-nurse
Safe in her hug.

I met a seller of shoe-laces
Down an alley in the bazaar
He wanted to sell me laces
But I have no shoes
Red laces, black laces
Laces of cotton and silk
He did not notice that I was bare-foot
He must have been either blind or mad
Or, perhaps, he was wise
We greeted each other
With the sign that is called 'You Know'
And both of us laughed.

Daughter of a bawd
Grand-daughter of bawds
Wife of a pimp
I was walking beside you
When you met a man in the street
I may have been ten years old or fourteen
I don't remember exactly
I suppose, mother, he gave you something
To me he offered a gold dinar
I knocked it out of his hand
So that it landed among the dogs
Whereupon he drew his dagger
And held it to my breast
I let him do as he liked
Then he went away, I don't know whither.

## Guzla

I received a look from a window
That faced north
A look from an overhanging oriel
Of carved wood –
Like the Bird-in-the-Cage
Hanging outside the house
The prisoner of Yourself

Life is Difficult
and Death is not Otherwise

To the bird the cage is not a reality
It does not comprehend it
Its vision only takes in what is useful to it
What birds find edible
It does not see anything else –
And I only see what I need for my needle-work

Life is Difficult
And Death is not Otherwise:
For space it has only a few square feet
But even that much is Distance
The cage of the Bird is its own Being
As my body is my Grating
Of which you made a gridiron
But my cries rose no higher
In proportion to my body weight
Than the cries of the birds to theirs –
Our Life is Difficult
And our Death is not Otherwise

A look from an oriel facing north
Also taught me the language of the birds
Some say that birds are Souls
Tell me, tell me, a word in the birds' language
That means *Nothing, of Nothing*!
Tell me that word, Soul of my Soul!

No, when they speak to each other
Souls are no different from birds
Nor birds different from souls
Our ears require
A multitude of words
Of carefully articulated sounds
So that what is said may be received
For birds a few suffice
Only varying in their tone of eagerness
And varying in their stress.

Do not wonder, do not wonder
Concerning the image you see:
Concerning the lips that shape themselves
Concerning the eyes that ask
Concerning the changing colours of the skin
Shimmering faintly in the dim light
Concerning the cheeks that fade –
What you have seen just now is yourself
Yourself in the mirror of a man.

That I was to experience you
That I knew
But not in such a desolation
Of mountains with thundering voices
Rushing down headlong from Taurus
As if driven by gales
Having been set free from captivity
I thought it must be some new trick
Devised by the bawd
And I felt afraid
I no longer wanted to act the heroine
Having learned the courage
Which is called humility.

Your eyes are glowing
With the red wine:
How shall I extinguish their glow?
– Only by drinking from them both
With kisses
One and one after the other –
Then you fill them up again
With the yellow wine
Which I love the most.

It is true, as you said, that I am dark
But the veil has a hem of silver
I said: 'I am your mirror, your mirror.'
And now I say:
These Turkmenian eyes
Are narrow as knives
Quivering in the wood at which they have been flung
Close to the temples, under the arm-pits
So that a man stands nailed to the wall

These eyes looking downwards
Cheek bent towards cheek
Pouring tenderness over a child
Like a hive of wild honey

I am your child, nailed to the wall
And resting in your lap
I am your child and I shine
Close around me, rays
Stand quivering like knives
I shine because your eyes are dark
And because you are so dark.

My vase was deeper than the vase of the Goddess of Love
And as empty in itself
But now, when someone unknown has placed in it a rose
A greater member than it can hold
Now I do not know how to acknowledge the child
Deep in my womb
It was said to be begotten by a Man of Light
But just before, I slept with Darkness
I, daughter of man, have borne twins
By different fathers
One evil, one good
And I cannot tell the difference between them.

Birth is simple:
You become you
Death is simple:
You are no longer you
It might have been the other way round
As in a mirror world:
Death could have borne you
And life extinguished you
– One way is as good as the other –
And perhaps it is that way:
It is from Death that you have emerged
And Life is slowly effacing you.

## The Lover

It was neither the sun, nor the moon, nor the stars
That gave me light
But the darkness
And love's light within me
Its rays that pierced my body

As if I were nobody
You, you, Fatumeh, you gave
My soul a shadow
A silver lamp you gave me
After you had gone.

Eyes leaning over me in the darkness
A darkness of a thousand eyes
And a thousand dizzy spaces
Darker than my eyebrows
Or the curls about my temples
Dimly seen, like a glimmer from an invisible lamp
A glow over cheek and forehead

It is the face of your beloved
Bent motionless over your fate
But why such hard eyes?

I know, after all, that the mirror is there
And that somebody completely different looks out from
    the mirror
Someday you will turn your eyes towards it
When you turn away again, I, too, will have vanished.

You are the witness of your own sorrow, your own desire
Your own mirror and, at the same time, your image in the
    mirror
More closely entwined and dependent upon each other
Than two lovers are. Hither the noise of the Knight
Battling the Dragon does not penetrate: in the void between
    you
Silence reigns, the silence of the eternal beholder
And of the eternally beheld, of virgin and mystic:
That love of yourself which is not selfish
Of yourself who loved to mirror yourself.

Love is a surgeon
Love can cut into your flesh like a scalpel
Love can operate upon your heart
Love can circumcise you
Perhaps you don't believe it
But I know. Love operates
Upon your skin, your hair, your gait
For Love there is no remedy
Except the surgeon's scalpel.

For how long, Angel
Are you going to keep on waking me
From these thoughts?
How many times are you going to wake me
Who have fallen asleep from them?

At times I have dreamt that I was your wife
At times, even, that I was your daughter
Who prostituted herself at the fairs
To win bread for us all

Once, though
I ran my fingers over your shoulder
And felt how the feathers
The down of the wings, melted away under them
Once I ran them over your cheek
Only to feel it crumble to powder
Like a butterfly's wing

How can I be rid of you?
Enough. Wake me no more with dreams.

As a rule what I felt was indifference
If not loathing or disgust
But you, Prince, gave me wings
Or are you a Djinn or a Genius
With you I flew up and up
Into super-celestial spheres
And you did not let me tumble headlong to earth
As anyone else would do –
No, on your wings
You lowered me gently down
On to my bed.

Who has experienced it
And who has not experienced it
The moment when suddenly
Everything becomes uncanny?
The voices and the footsteps in the alley are hushed
As though behind closed windows and doors
Though these stand open
The senses are numbed
And the object you were holding in your hand
Falls silently to the ground
The colours flow into one another
Change their appearance, their shimmer
Like little dice in a crap-game
Deep in a peep-show of darkness.
The presence of someone is felt
Someone who does not exist
Yet is the cause of all this.

## Joachim and Anna

So is portrayed the meeting
Of the Blessed Joachim and the Blessed Anna
So is depicted her meeting with him
Each came from a different angel with the same message
And the angels could still be seen
On the gold ground in the upper corners of the picture
He advanced from one city-gate, she from another
To meet in an open space in the centre
In front of the embrasured wall of a palace
How eagerly she flew into his arms
And laid her hands on his breast
How her mantle fluttered red behind her
In the rushing movement
How she raised her face
Expressing a grave joy
A look of affection. For whom?
For him? For herself?
With affection confronting her fate
That fate which was her hope

And Joachim received her
His mantle fluttering green behind him
With his left hand he supported her right elbow
And lightly pressed with his right foot
On her left slipper of red morocco.

*Joasaph and Fatumeh*


Do you see this alley?
Between long low walls
Walls without windows
But with now and again a door
A low one
All along the alley lie heaps of garbage
Down the middle there runs a drain
Or a gutter
With a dead cat in it
A few live cats can also be seen, roaming about
And a starved stray dog with protruding ribs
Nozzling the garbage
But except for these no one, nothing
Now notice carefully
Before the moon is hidden by clouds
The green little wooden door on the right
Grope your way forward until you reach it
It seems to open by itself
And now you find yourself in a garden
What does it matter that you cannot see the trees
You can hear them whispering
What does it matter that you cannot see the flowers
You can smell them
What does it matter that you cannot see the fountain
Or its widening circles of pearly bubbles
You can hear it splashing
What does it matter that you cannot see the wind
You can feel it blowing towards you
And the fluttering of her light robe
Which is billowing out behind her

Because she is running in haste
And now you feel her hands on your breast
Appealing to you
With her right hand she supports your left elbow
With her left foot she touches your right
And her face expresses an affection which is also fate
For you sense that it is looking up into yours
Filled with its fate

Both have advanced through the darkness
He from his shadow-angel, she from hers
He from his gate, she from hers
So was Prince Joasaph's meeting
With me, Fatumeh.

But the name
Of him who was born of our meeting
If you want to know that
You must ask the young Prince
Who embraces a jar

In my fate, Fatumeh
Lies my hope
I shall not live
If you should die.

I thought for a long time
Of her
Who was beautiful
With an unfamiliar beauty
O my Imām!
You sent me a sign of Paradise
No more extraordinary than the quick glance of a bird
But a sign nevertheless
My gratitude shall be greater than your gift
My sign a great one
Greater than yours
Someone greater than you touched me
Thus I felt as slowly
Slowly I walked along
Waiting to be caught up with
And led by the hand
Into one alley, then out into another
The first bread that I eat
Shall be an offering to you.

# Xoanon*

In you I possess a miracle-working Icon
If to possess is to possess nothing:
As she possesses me, so I possess her.
She was given to me on the day she 'revealed herself'
At a time and place decided upon beforehand
And the same Panayía is revealed
Whenever the heart so wishes. Supported by her arm
On a footstool in receding perspective
Stands a grown-up baby in princely swaddling-clothes
Who is the last Prince of my line
I remove him, for everything that pertains
To this Panayía is removable
As a robber can wrench
The silver-smith's basmá† from some image
With smoke-blackened hands and worn away by kisses
I remove the crown, I remove the two angels
The annunciators of bliss
From the clouds and the gold ground in the upper corners
I unfasten the jewelled clasp of the Maphorion‡
And remove the veil from the hair and the neck
I relax the creases over her right breast
And the creases over the left
Gently, to ease the pain. I remove like a spider's web
The thin under-garment that leaves the riddle
Both solved and unsolved, and she looks at me
The eyes brown in the bluish-white of the eyeballs

* *Xoanon*: ancient wooden image in Greek temples, i.e. an icon.
† *Basmá*: the shield (protection) of silver covering certain icons completely, except for faces and hands.
‡ *Maphorion*: head-dress, veil.

Steadfastly look at me. I remove the arms
The brown hand with its rose, and the brown breasts
The right breast first, then the left, but gently
To ease the pain, then the scalp and the cheeks
And the girdle after having kissed it
And lastly the big eyes which look at me
Steadfastly look at me still
After they have been removed
I remove the gold ground and the ground coat
Until the thick-veined wood is exposed
A piece of old olive wood, saved long ago
Out of a storm-felled tree
On some coast way up in the north. In the wood
Almost hidden, an eye, the eye-knot of a twig
That must have been broken off when the tree was still
    young
You look at me. Hodigítria.* Philoúsa.†

  * *Hodigítria*: the woman who leads; a type of madonna on the
icon.
  † *Philoúsa*: the one who loves (or kisses); a type of madonna on
the icon.

Your face is mourning
A bitter line round the mouth
The eyes veiled
You are mourning
But not the son you have lost
You are mourning your own loneliness
Therefore
The eyes of all the lonely are turned
Lonely One, towards you

Your solitude's grief
Is our solitude's desire.

To suffer is difficult
To suffer without loving is difficult
To love without suffering is impossible
To love is difficult.

## The Harem at Erechtheion

Those knowing eyes look at me
Steadfastly without blinking
They give me their glances
Before they vanish
At every moment
They look at me with their look

You put your hand under her veil
Under her mantle
And touch the dagger
The hilt of the dagger under her left breast
A little to one side
In the crease just under the breast
You see and, seeing, you know
That everything is turning to ashes
That your look is changing
And soon will cease to be
Yet there remains –
The golden light of evening through the open door
And the evening's ashes –

A prince who shall remain nameless
Kneels and embraces me
An urn whose shape is feminine
Like his own shapes

You ask: What is in the urn
That this young prince is embracing
Kneeling before it, as if it were a burnt-offering
Why in his crown should there burn
A fire of Kashmir wool that has been dyed red?
Why, on his upper-lip, only lightly shaded
Does the gentle trait remain?
Why, at his feet, does the brazier smoulder
Sending up smoke-coils of a pleasing fragrance
Which look like the folds of his garment
Or the veil which he has wrapped around the urn?
Why do the branches of the trees bless him
And why are they ever green? Why do the birds
Hidden in the bushes lament
As if they were asking: Who is in there?

For everything in this image has faded already
And the smoke-coils of incense were dispersed by the wind
Long ago. What is left lingers like mist
A want without object, and without anyone
Who still wants anyone. But such a mist

Can also be the sign of the Shadow
The Shadow that lives without Sun and Moon
She is there, he is there
In the depths of an urn
Even were the urn broken to pieces.

A hush fell on the evening, as if everybody
Was expecting something

The blind one asked: 'Habibi, what are the stars saying?'
She answered: 'In the Milky Way I see a big bag of snow
A blank patch – that forebodes bad weather.'
Again he asked: 'What are the stars saying?'
'They twinkle, their light is unsteady
Such stars forebode tempests and earthquakes . . .'
Yet again he asked: 'Habibi, what are the stars saying?'
'Water has gathered around them
Their darting rays are their tears
For this has already come to pass:
Roofless people are fleeing along the roads
Or squatting in the cold around brush-wood fires
Yes, some have cut down the holy olive-trees
Which gave them nourishment
To nourish the fire
And support life for a little longer.'

On this market-place which is called the Square of the Wall
Stands a black statue
Which can be seen from all sides
A round Shadow
And the square itself
Paved with closely set white stones, cemented together
Is a horizontal wall
Around the square run the walls of a palace
Which is called the Palace of the Middle
Walls that are vertical streets
White-washed down to the mud
The swarm of flat shadows you see
On these streets which are walls are people
But the Square of the Wall is always empty
Except for the black statue in the middle
Should anyone, man or woman, dare to walk there
He or she becomes a shadow upon
The surrounding walls which are streets.

Through the aimless dark
Again I walked last night
With a lantern in my hand
– Or was it through aimless side-streets?
However I held the lantern
The shadow I saw extended itself
As if it were my own
It tried to feel its way
But only grew longer and longer
Till at last there were only my feet
Feeling their way through the darkness:

The Unevenness
And the Stones which lay in my way
Seemed to be lying in wait for my feet!
I have a bad foot, which is the good one
I have a good foot, which is the one that tries to walk
Right Foot, you kick aside Left Foot
Left Foot, you kick aside Right Foot
And still the stones
Lie quietly there
Stones! You cast long Shadows
Across my path to Her.

At the hour of transformation, the hour
When the veil of Time is rent asunder
I hear a Song
A traditional air
As a mother, The Mother, sings it
So was her cradle-song
Yes, thus it was:
Come to me, come
Come home! A dish of nourishing yoghurt
Freshly made, is waiting for you.
Come! Take a spoonful!
Come! Take another spoonful!

You, who at this hour make much of me
Would you forgive me
With tiny hands
I push away your spoonfuls
And you will put your arms around me
Shedding frozen tears.

Stood upon auction-blocks
In the market of Isfahān
A thousand and one bodies
A thousand and one souls
Were put up to auction as slaves
And a thousand and one merchants
Made various bids for various souls and bodies

The souls were like women
The bodies were like men
And the Merchant was lucky
Well-repaid for his acumen
Who managed to make off with
A soul and a body
That matched and could be mated.

Life is sad
And shrinks before these brutal glances
Life in me is sad
Life is sad
Hemmed in by this crowd
Of eyes which tell you everything
What they desire and what they do not desire

By the stream of voices
In which the only necessary one
Is the voice of the water-seller
Rising above the host of eyes which tell you everything
And for that reason nothing

These inner eyes
This inner voice
Which is also the voice of the water-seller:
'Drink this water,' he sings
'It is good.'

You, my Beloved
Who have only one voice
Not many

Here I still walk in the noisy alleys
Seeking consolation from the criers
Who sell everything, and letting them buy
Anything from me they like

But beyond the noise
As from a distant mountain, I hear you
In whose arms I should have liked to die
Your voice calling, singing a song
About my Fate since I lost you
The eternal cradle-song you have become for me.

The arms of my shadow grope along the wall
The wall where your shadow stands motionless
Ever since you left me
With taunts that were my own
Only when I have calmed myself
And let my arms fall
Does my shadow melt into your shadow
And my hands meet
Behind your back
Only then
In this moment of embrace
Does the wall again become white
And the moon comes with its brush and pail
Of chalk whitewash
And with borrowed light
Paints over something which has never been.

It is the dark that contains all the colours
Not the light
Even if it be the saffron-yellow for a bride
Or the blood-red for a harlot
What else are colours but shadows
Or shades of light?
Lay colours on top of each other and you get black
The purest vision
Is pure shadow
The opposite of light

If you look right into the sun
Or a white-hot iron
And then shut your eyes
Only then will you see colour
The true colour of the blood
Which is your own, inward

Dark, tarnished are all colours
Except the black
Which can never become darker
In it you see me.

I have received Nothing
The inhuman Nothing I sought.
Flecked with black and white were the wings of the
    archangel
Who stood on guard
And now stands threatening
Over us, for whom
Sleep is far away
Pain lies here
I am lying with you, Fatumeh
Whose paralysed body is pressed against mine
In an embrace without end:
Neither of us can move
Neither caress the other

Only your eyes, looking deep
Into my eyes, are lost
Yes, though the darkness is all-powerful
We see each other
Eyes looking into eyes as deeply
As is possible for two people

– You, lover of women!
– You, beloved of men!

I am a black woman
With a white child in my arms
Go to sleep! Go to sleep
Sleep, little one, sleep
But you are fretful
Do you want the breast?
Sleep, go to sleep
I weep for you
The white child is dying
The white child is dead
I understand nothing
The white child does not want to take the breast
I will warm you against my stomach
Cradle you in my lap
Kiss your eyes one after the other
To see if you will open them
I understand nothing
This child is dead
What shall I, a simple woman
Do with this white child?
I have no right even to bury it

– Look away, go away, you dog!
You understand nothing.

You who had seemed too familiar to yourself
Came to a city where the noises on all sides
Made you a stranger to yourself
Your life worth nothing
Begin from the beginning
When you have nothing to begin with
Except the End
Which you wished were different –

The streams of words without
Like the streams of blood within
A ground-swell of estrangement
Now I know
That everything is as it is everywhere:
The same feeling of discomfort
At conditions that grow even harder
The rewards for your services each day less
In the end completely inadequate
In this market our numbers increase steadily
Soon we shall be too many
Unable to carry on with so few customers
And only he will be welcome to the mystery
Who seeks it within himself

# Karagöz

The Shadow on the wall of cloth
Is always your neighbour's, the image
Of your neighbour's concern for herself
Her sagging breasts, her barren sex
And the shadow on this image, another
You yourself, alone and young
– At the door of the guest-house
Stands someone who raises and lowers her lamp
I watch my shadow
Growing shorter or longer
Or broken into fragments by the tree-branches.

You have the face of a dwarf-woman
With blue eyes, evil eyes
You are ugly and deformed
But what shall a man do
If not amuse himself?
The child you will bring forth
Between your stunted legs
Will not live
Because I shall disown it

Angel! Forgive him and me
Who to satisfy my hunger
Must love at any price
Even the lowest.

Your head breathes slowly and heavily, Fatumeh
Expands and contracts
As if it felt the heaviness
Of its own weight on the pillow –
The long threads of your thoughts
And the tendrils of your thinking
Your spring was blue, with a streak of red
Red was your summer
And blood-red is now your autumn
You are like the jelly-fish
Flowering red in death
Trailing its long threads behind it
Your head tries to breathe
As you lie in the ripples on the shore
With scarcely enough water
To rise and fall in
There is no depth any longer
And no hope – Or is there still?
Yes, a hope of sinking into one's own depth of jelly
When the sea withdraws
And one is left on the sand
To shrink
And turn hard as stone.

I travel from market to market
What else shall an old woman do
Who has to paint her face white!
One night there were five Pechenegues*
They were dirty
O, you should have seen it, my Arab
You would have pulled out your dagger
And killed yourself
You were always so particular about keeping clean
But it is better that you are dead
Than that I am alive
I should not have liked to see myself
In the calm mirrors of your eyes
You were lucky to die by a dagger
Or did you in fact
Throw yourself over a precipice?
I cannot even have the good fortune to die
I see you, I see you, a long way off
We shall never meet again
For you are in heaven
With plenty of food and many women
And I am on earth with many men
It's enough to pay for sour milk and bread.

    * *Pechenegues*: nomads from the later Völkerwanderung Age.

Your face covered
With blood and dirt
You lay in the street
And the richly dressed
Who passed you by
These, in rich garments
Of silver, of gold
Their eyes looking straight ahead
In the right direction
Composed the gold ground for your face
As you lay in the street
Covered with blood and dirt.

The tale is never ending
It begins where it ends
And man is imprisoned in the same circle
A man, a woman
An evil, a good
A Mother. A Father.
A Daughter. A Brother.
A bird with observant eyes
Flits from branch to branch
And watches you –
Who is the bird?
Your Soul
The lives of birds are hard:
They look at you and are afraid.

See what is left you
Of Soul, of Spirit
You can count the days and the years
Maybe four, maybe five –
What sort of time is that?
And then you will appear
In the Square
Exactly on time
No one will meet you
No matter how far the finger of the sundial turns

No one has given birth to you, no one
This meeting you arranged when you gave birth to
    yourself
Then, too, your Shadow
Gave birth to No one.

You whose body is in such dire want
How can you endure?
Doubly tormented
By a want within and a want from without

Love and Friendship walked by
Arm in arm and said:
Truly
Her life is a thin membrane
Stretched taut like a drum-skin
Between this and That –
The mere touch of a finger
The mere flick of a nail
Sets her vibrating
As if she were alive

Thus with over-tones I accompany
The rhythm of your voice, its choked wailing
And the strum of your fingers
On that single string.

I saw a coffin, draped in green, being borne from Eyub
By ten, by a hundred, by a thousand relatives and friends
How is it possible, you may ask, for such a multitude
To act as bearers for one coffin of average human length?
Oh, that's easy, that lightens the burden:
The pair at the tail of the procession keep hurrying forward
To relieve the pair at its head
Who shift their hold and become the second pair
Then the third, then the fourth, as a new pair come to the
    front
After ranking as chief mourners, they take second place and
    so on
Until, by and by, they rank as cousins twice removed
And so on until they come to the rear and the process
    begins again
In this way the last shall always be first.
Death's number is even, life's is odd.
That is why the one they bear is the thousand-and-First.

Is there really any difference
Between Day and Night?
How blind we are when our eyes are open
How perceptive we are when we close them in sleep.

You lived out all your Day
And became a blear-eyed hag!
While still in your youth
You were thrust into a Night that was not everlasting
But alive with images, visions, desires!
What, then, is Day? What, then, is Night?
Breasts wizened or breasts full?
It is all the same!
Then who am I?
Fatumeh, who lift myself up
And fall and rise again.

You are seen, you see – for a short while
You feel and are felt – for a short while also
You are seen, I feel. But for just how long?
Perhaps the end is already here.
But I remember that the Nightingale has sung
Seven by seventy times
In groves, in forests, on mountains
In the everlasting Night which is drawing near
This Song it shall be that makes us One.

Richly endowed in my flesh
I was selfish but faithful
On occasion you found me obstinate
And could not bear it
Now I am a skeleton
But a beautiful one
With joints well set in their sockets
If you are a Prince with a Prince's powers:
Then put muscles upon me
Intestines into my belly
Slip over me a wonderful skin
That shimmers like silk
And speak to my heart
Otherwise, my bones of glass
Will ring for you in the wind
Bells of dead glass tinkle in the garden
For you to take between your teeth.
If you are a clever juggler, you may chew on them for ever
If a skilful joiner you shall always
Have slivers of glass in your finger-tips
If a true lover, we shall meet when you are dead.

I call you to mind
Call you up out of the grave!
Once you washed off me
My memories of me
All my memories of myself
So, someday I shall wash off you
Your memory, your memories of me
So that nothing may stand between us.

Long have I watched your shadow, Fatumeh
Watched it through sunny days and moonlit nights
It was so black that the wall around it
Gave it a silver outline
Which glittered as cunningly as a basmá*
Whether I approached, whether I withdrew
However I tried to blot you out
With some shadow of my own
You remained visible
And the silver around you
Untarnished
Dark One, Light's Twin
I learned to walk round you
Regard you from every angle
Round as a woman
The light which made you dark
And the silver about you glitter
That light was within me, as love
But not *my* love. No!
Straight through me shone the Sun and the Moon
And only Your shadow gave my soul
Substance and Presence.

* See note, page 107.

## End of Tale of Fatumeh

'Beloved, shall we meet at your place or at mine?'
So echoed her mocking question in the Night
'At yours!' So echoed his mocking answer
Once more they wandered through the Night
Far out of the City, far beyond the suburbs
Over the oasis gardens, up out of the Night
The red dawn rose. Further on the road
Lost itself in the sand, in the Sun
That climbed higher out of the Night
The Moon turned pale. The Sun cast darker shadows
As it set they came to her place. In the Night
All roads had vanished. They lay down beside each other
Beneath him nothing was to be seen of her Shadow
But when they shifted positions as lovers will
Nothing was to be seen under his Shadow
Thus the Night became a Day and the Day again a Night.

Moon! Moon!★ so might a poor farmer's wife see you
When, having driven one furrow with her wooden plough
She raises her face
And wipes the sweat from her forehead
Before starting upon the next one

– Are you an egg in space
A hen's egg with a wrinkled shell
Or are you a wind egg that dimly mirrors
Our fields and mountains?

But the angel grips her arm
And points to where
A Star has just fallen
Leaving an empty space
Inside the Moon's sickle.


★ In this poem we have an example of how elements from music
and art fused into a unity of their own. The original poem begins
with 'Avgó! Avgó!', and has here been translated 'Moon! Moon!'
Ekelöf was a great fan of Boris Christoff's interpretations of Mous-
sorgsky's song cycles, and played some of his recordings over and
over again. On the day when I had an appointment with Ekelöf at
his home at Sigtuna, he was tired and tense. Almost the only subject
he could converse on with any flair at all was music, and whichever
way the conversation turned, it always came back to Moussorgsky;
when this topic was exhausted, the conversation started over again
with this marvellous bass, Boris Christoff (Ekelöf had seen Chalia-
pin in Paris in the early thirties). The session ended with Ekelöf
playing LP records of children's songs by Moussorgsky. He hummed
and gesticulated, deeply moved. When the music finally became less
emotional, he lay back on his bed, his face became peaceful, and

he fell asleep, while the music of Moussorgsky continued. One of his favourites was a lullaby with a recurring phrase 'Bajú! Bajú!' (Lull! Lull!), which Ekelöf heard as 'Avgó! Avgó!', thus associating it with the Greek word for 'egg'. In his imagination Ekelöf identified this song 'Avgó!' with a reproduction of a fresco from a Serbian church, in which an angel standing before an old shepherd points up towards the sky, his arm around the shepherd's shoulders. The old man looks up with pious awe. In the picture there is neither egg nor moon! But the poet made the Russian 'Bajú!' into the Greek 'Avgó!', then made his egg into a moon: moved by the shepherd's simple piety, and his own profound experience before the sublimity of the scene, Ekelöf sang 'Avgó! Avgó!' Later he went on to make the old shepherd into an old woman, thereby further underscoring the female dominance – the almost frenzied devotion to women – in *The Tale of Fatumeh*.